Dedicated to Robert J. Rubin, "Bob" — my soul mate and best friend — who lived life to the fullest during his near 7½ year journey with brain cancer, and to William Clifford Heinz, the adoring 4-year-old grandson, who unconditionally loved and helped his dear "Bobbo," posed for pictures and helped write the this book.

Honor Bob with a donation to the Dr. Marnie Rose Foundation:
www.DrMarnieRose.org • 5300 N. Braeswood Blvd., #4-350, Houston, TX 77096

Will & Bobbo

Text © 2016 Marlene Rubin and William Clifford Heinz
Illustrations © 2016 Christina Mattison Ebert

All rights reserved. No part of this book may be reproduced, transmitted or stored in any information retrieval system in any form or by any means, graphic, electronic or mechanical, including photocopying, taping, recording—except in the case of brief quotations embodied in critical articles or reviews—without written permission from the holder of the copyright.

Typeset in Spinnaker
Cover title typeset in Myriad Std Tilt

Back cover photo: Gary Maltz Photography

ISBN: 978-0-692-6646-7-4

I am Will.

This is my Bobbo.
My Bobbo was diagnosed with brain cancer.

Here he is with my Mahmoo.
For 4 ½ years, Bobbo lived a fairly normal life.

We still did fun things together.
We saw an Astros baseball player.

I went to swim therapy with him and got a red icy drink. We even saw a pirate show!

He watched me play with my marble toy.

He watched a rodeo parade with my family.

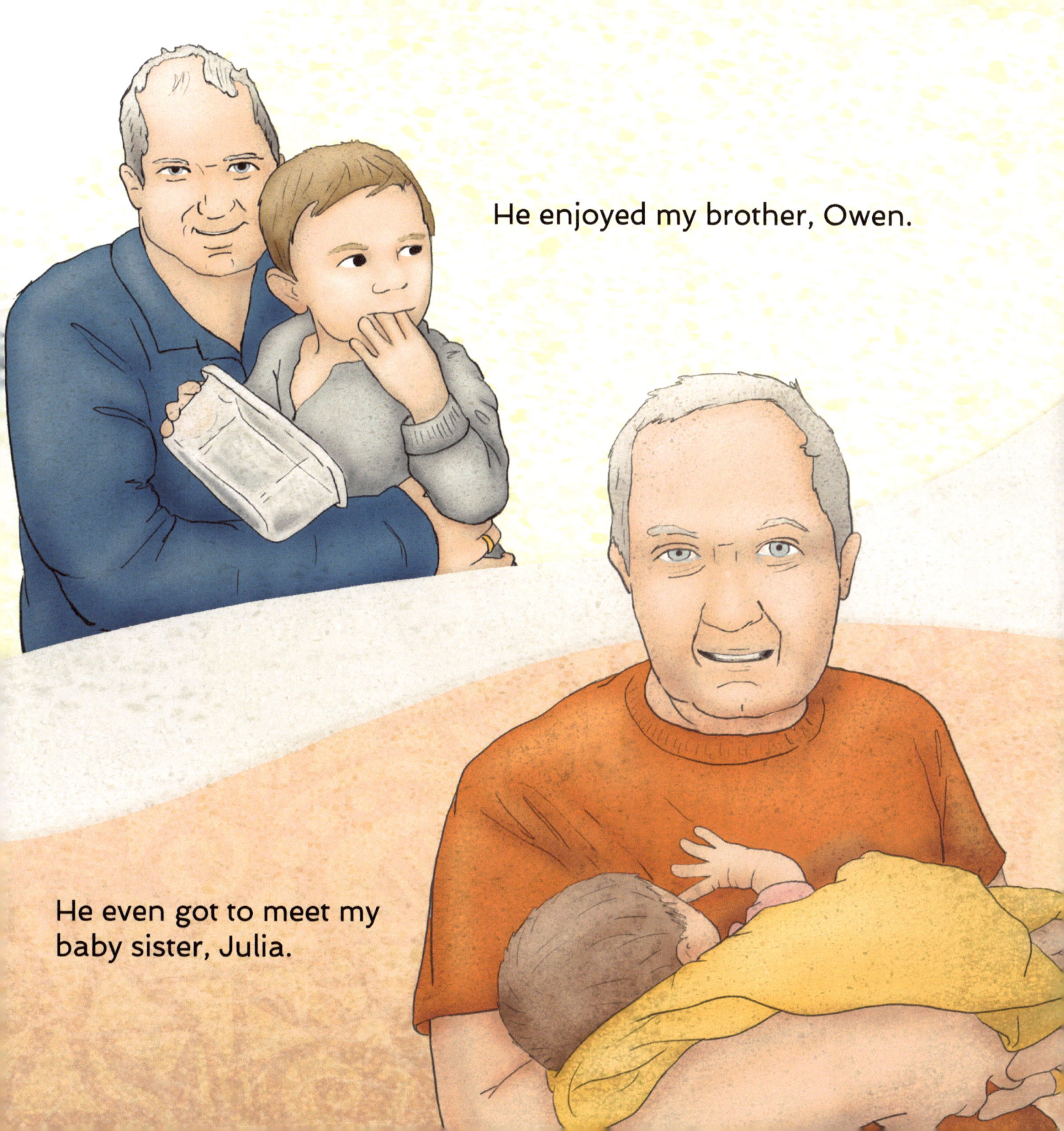

He enjoyed my brother, Owen.

He even got to meet my baby sister, Julia.

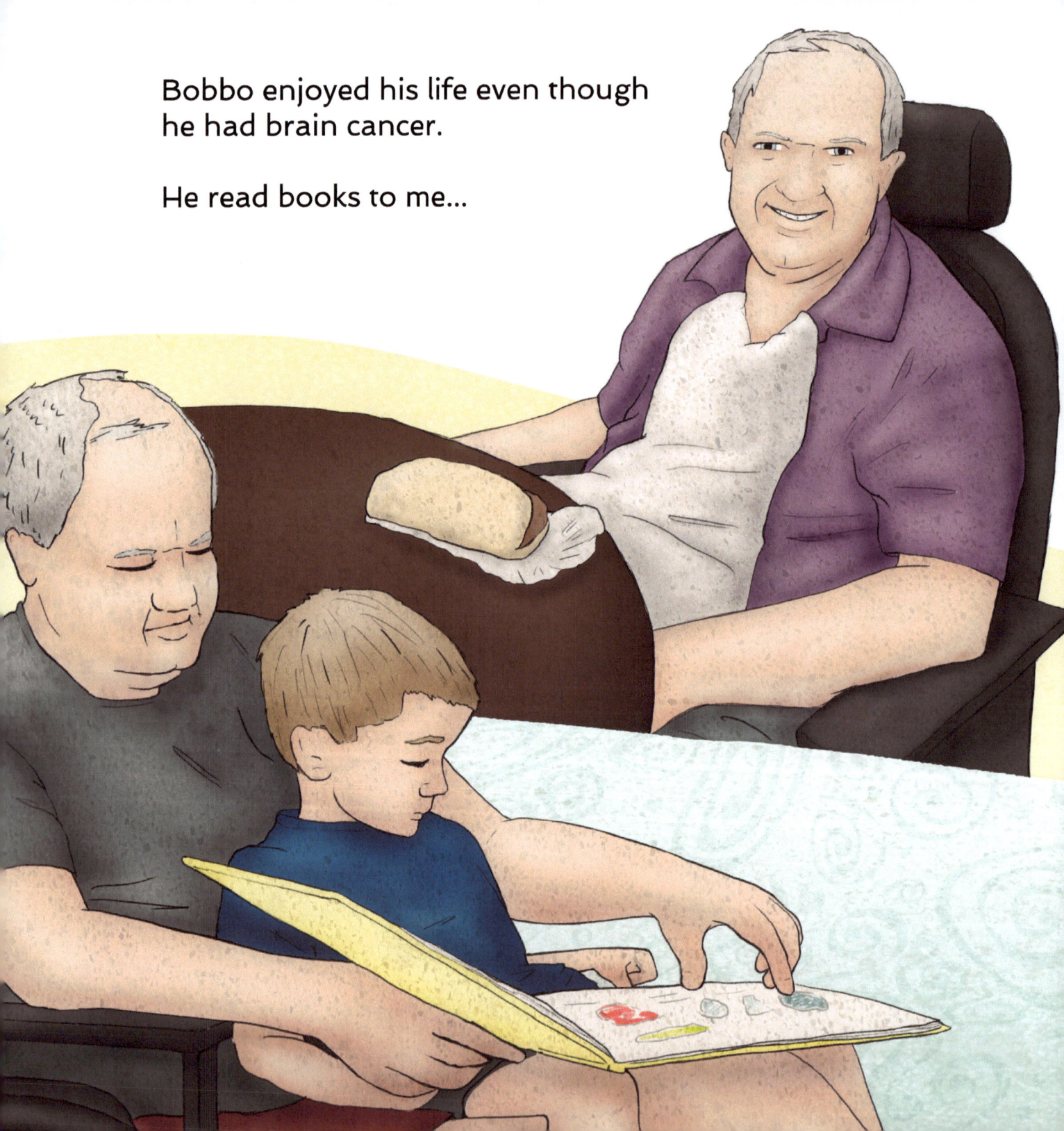

Bobbo enjoyed his life even though he had brain cancer.

He read books to me...

...he went on a farm tour and visited the Baseball Hall of Fame.

He dressed up to watch a wedding on the internet.

He traveled to Europe and went on a road trip to California.

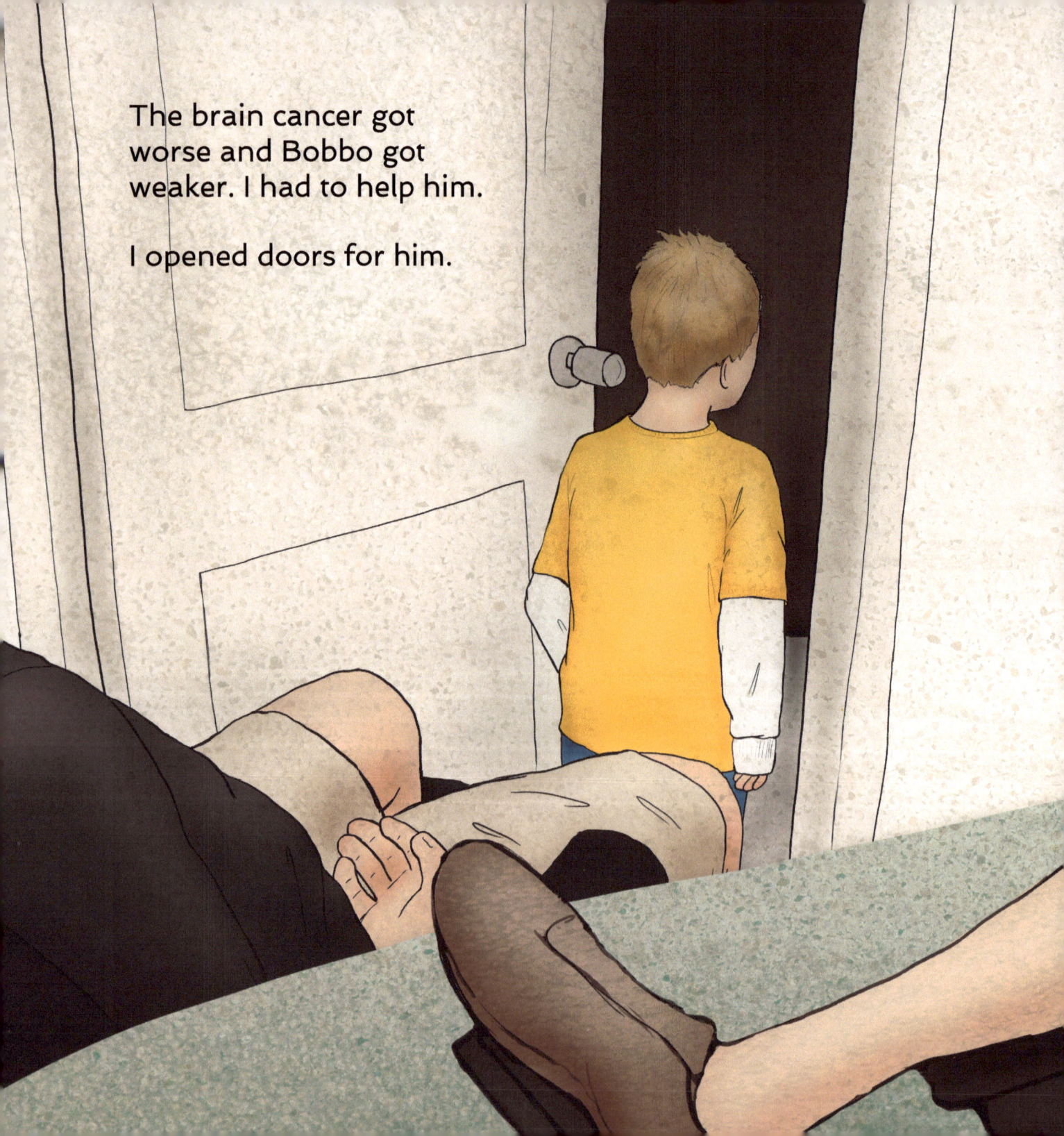

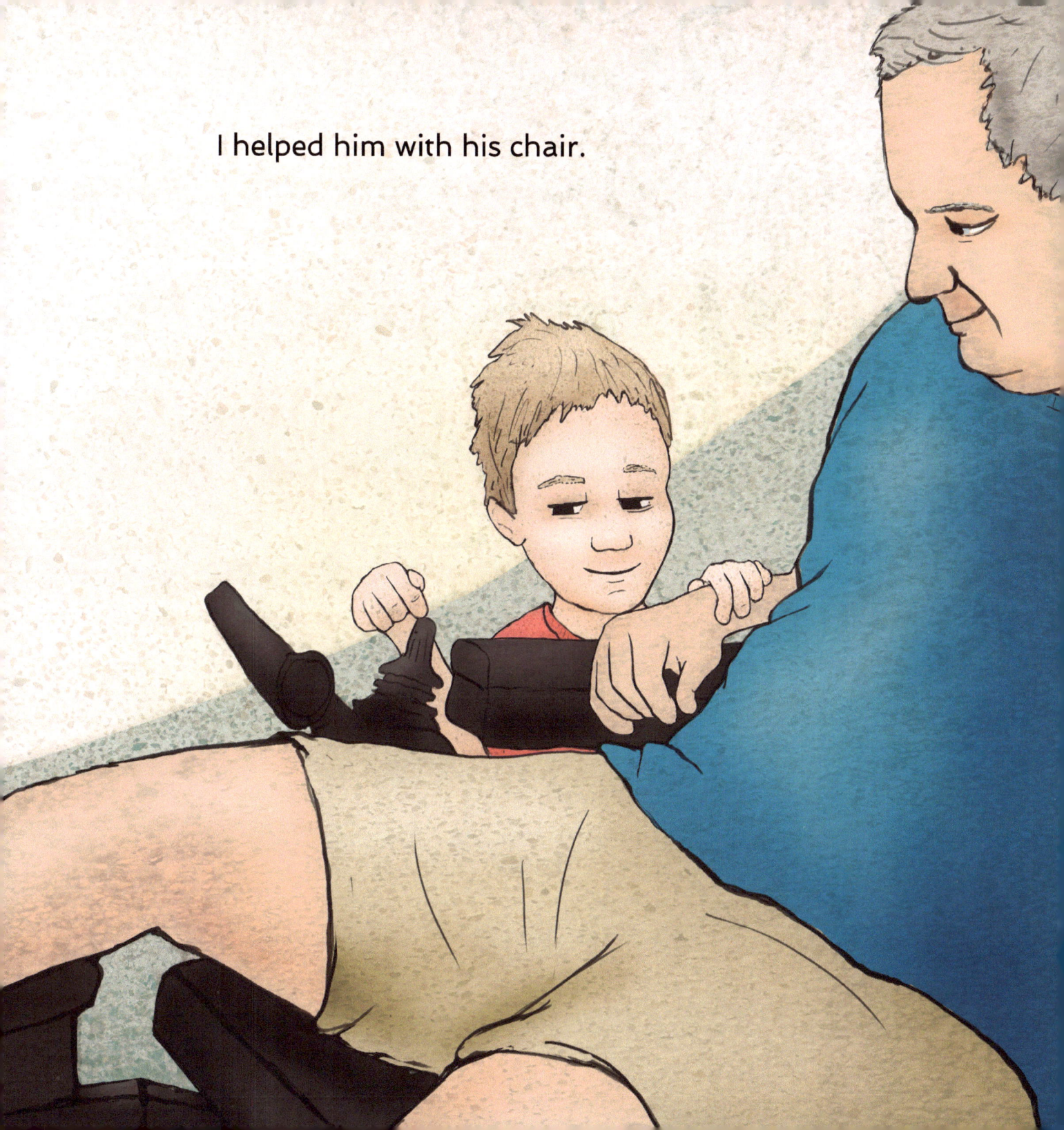

I fed Bobbo when he was too weak.

I helped him move his legs.

My brother and I made a play meerkat to sleep with Bobbo at night.

The meerkat says, "I love you," when you squeeze its hand.
He liked it.

Bobbo died. I was sad.

I remember all the wonderful times I had with him.

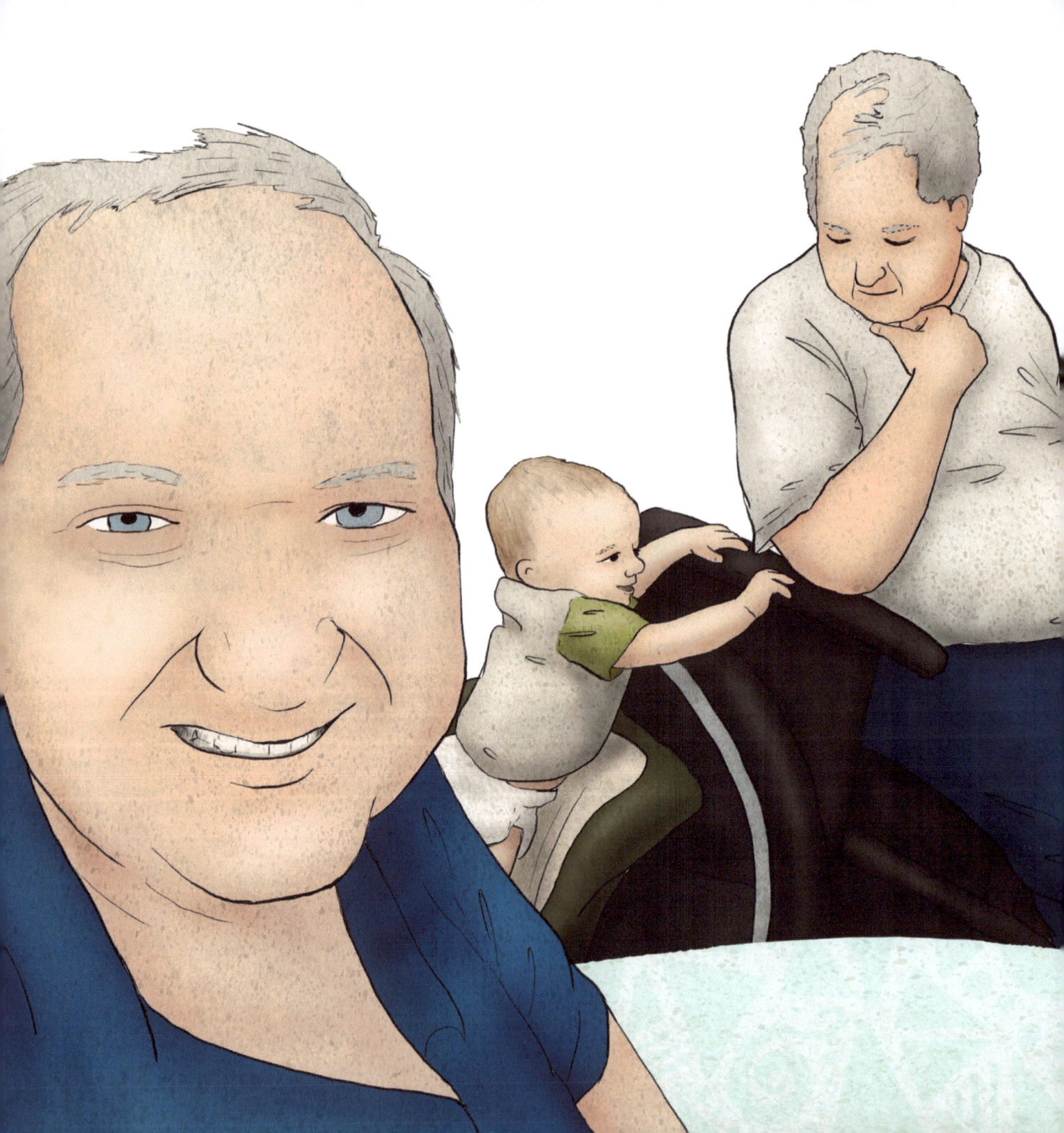

Bobbo loved golf, but best of all, he loved to be with his family.

He was a doctor who was recognized as exceptional.
Here I am with the medical school book
that Bobbo gave me. It's heavy!

Mahmoo made this book so I can always remember Bobbo.
He wanted to watch me grow up.

I will make him proud.

www.ingramcontent.com/pod-product-compliance
Lightning Source LLC
Chambersburg PA
CBHW041232040426
42444CB00002B/132